Football's
CLEVER
QUARTERBACKS

Football's
CLEVER
QUARTERBACKS

Richard Rainbolt

Lerner Publications Company
Minneapolis

ACKNOWLEDGMENTS   **745**

The illustrations are reproduced through the courtesy of: pp. 6, 44, 52, 55, 57, 59, 61, 64, 67, 69, 71, Vernon J. Biever; pp. 11, 14, 21, 27, 30, 31, 42, Pro Football Hall of Fame; pp. 17, 19, Chicago Bears; pp. 23, 34, Los Angeles Rams; p. 37, Independent Picture Service; p. 39, New York Football Giants; p. 47, Baltimore Colts; p. 49, John E. Biever.

LIBRARY OF CONGRESS CATALOGING IN PUBLICATION DATA

Rainbolt, Richard.
    Football's clever quarterbacks.

    (The Sports Heroes Library)
    SUMMARY: Brief biographies emphasizing the careers of ten quarterbacks: Sammy Baugh, Sid Luckman, Bob Waterfield, Otto Graham, Norm Van Brocklin, Y. A. Tittle, Johnny Unitas, Bart Starr, Lenny Dawson, Joe Namath.

    1. Football—Biography—Juvenile literature. 2. Quarterback (Football)—Juvenile literature.   [1. Football—Biography. 2. Quarterback (Football)] I. Title.

GV939.A1R34   796.33′2′0922[B][920]   74-27467
ISBN 0-8225-1051-0

Published simultaneously in Canada by
J. M. Dent & Sons (Canada) Ltd., Don Mills, Ontario

Manufactured in the United States of America

International Standard Book Number: 0-8225-1051-0
Library of Congress Catalog Card Number: 74-27467

3   4   5   6   7   8   9   10   85   84   83   82   81   80   79

Contents

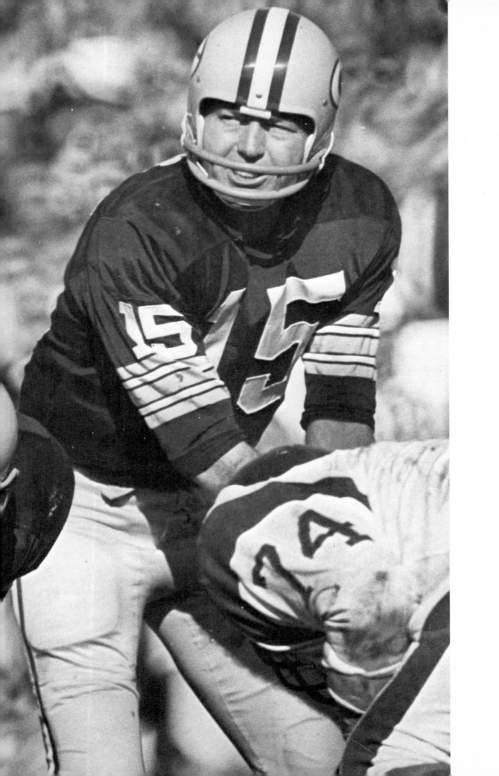

In the sport of professional (pro) football, the quarterback has become the most important player on the team. Quarterbacks today make more money than any other player. Some quarterbacks have become millionaires just because they could pass a football well.

This ability has not always been so important. In the early days of football, the forward pass was not used very often. But little by little, the professional teams began to look at the forward pass as a way to make quick scores. The coaches saw that passing was a good way to spread out the opposing defense. They also saw that their own running game worked better when they used the pass.

At first, passes were thrown by a player who was also a good runner. But this began to change in the late 1930s. At that time, Sammy Baugh and Sid Luckman started playing pro football. They were both good passers, even though they were not great runners.

Sammy Baugh was the first of the great passers. He was the man who made pro football the game that it is today. As the star of the Washington Redskins, Baugh proved that a team could win if it used the forward pass often during a game. After that, the other pro teams began to change their offensive formations to make better use of the pass.

One of these new formations was the T-formation, first used by the Chicago Bears. In the T-formation, the quarterback either handed the ball to another player or dropped back himself to throw a pass. To run this new formation, the Bears hired Sid Luckman. Luckman was a young man who could throw a football with great accuracy.

After Baugh and Luckman came other football greats, including Otto Graham and Bob Waterfield. Both of these men were good passers who led their teams to victory with a blend of running and passing.

Besides these four famous quarterbacks and the others included in this book, there have been other fine pro quarterbacks. They include Frankie Albert, Paul Christman, Tommy Thompson, Bobby Layne, Charlie Conerly, Eddie LeBaron, Tobin Rote, John Brodie, Sonny Jurgensen, Charlie Johnson, Frank Ryan, Don Meredith, and Roman Gabriel. Each of these men has added something to the game of professional football as we know it today. And each probably has his own fans who would claim that he should be rated the best in the game.

Whatever qualities make a good quarterback, there is one quality that they all have—each has been an outstanding passer. Some have been better than others in passing. Some have been good in calling plays, in leading the team, in kicking, or in all-around football skills. But all great quarterbacks have been great passers.

This book contains stories of some of the quarterbacks who have contributed the most to professional football. These athletes have helped make pro football the exciting sport that it is today.

Sammy Baugh

Sammy Baugh was a Texan who looked like what Texans are supposed to look like. He was a tall, thin man with a hawk-like face—the kind of man you might expect to see on a ranch. And that's just where Sam went when his football-playing days were over. But before he retired, Sam helped bring about great changes in one of America's favorite sports.

Sam Baugh is thought to have been the first of the great passers in professional football. Until Baugh arrived on the scene, pro football was mostly a running game. The forward pass was used only when nothing else worked. But by the time Baugh retired, the pass had become a necessary part of football.

Sam Baugh was born in Temple, Texas, in 1914. Though he was pretty good at sports as a boy, Sam did not have the natural ability to become a great athlete. But he did become a great athlete, mainly through practice.

In high school, Baugh played end on the football team until he was switched to the backfield. In those days—the early 1930s—most teams used the single wing formation. This formation required the man who received the ball to be a good runner, blocker, *and* passer. So Sam worked hard to develop these skills, especially passing. He practiced by throwing a football through an automobile tire that he had hung from a tree by a rope. Each time, he tried to throw the ball through the center of the tire without hitting the sides. Sam practiced this until he could do it regularly. Then he started throwing the football through the tire while it was swinging back and forth.

Sam also went out for the high-school baseball team. As it turned out, Sam showed more skill as a third baseman than he did as a football player. It was on a baseball scholarship that Baugh entered Texas Christian University in 1933. At the university, he played both baseball and football. But he did not become a star in football until his junior year. That year, his passing ability began to draw attention. By the end of his senior year, Baugh had become such a sensation that he was selected by most of the nation's All-America teams.

When he left college, Sam Baugh was offered a baseball contract by the St. Louis Cardinals and a football contract by the Washington Redskins. He decided to sign both contracts. But Sam's baseball career did not last long. His football injuries kept him from playing good baseball. Sam soon realized that a football career would be much better for him. So he went to training camp with the Redskins. From the time he got there, Baugh seemed to be changing the professional game. He started by testing the popular image of the big, burly football player. Standing only 6 feet, 1 inch tall and weighing only 175 pounds, Sam began mastering the game known for its big, strong running backs.

Baugh played his first pro game in 1937 against the powerful New York Giants. He completed 11 out of 16 passes that day to lead the Redskins to a 13-3 upset win. Through a combination of passing and running, Baugh guided his team to a division title that first year. Then, in the National Football League (NFL) championship game, he led the Redskins against the mighty Chicago Bears. Baugh threw three touchdown passes during the game's second half to give Washington the title.

Through his dedication to football, Sam became more than just a great passer. He played defense, too. Once, he set a record for pass interceptions — four in a single game. He taught himself to punt and became one of the greatest punters in football.

Sammy Baugh (left) with teammate Eddie LeBaron on the sidelines

Sam would stay after practice to work on his punting after the other players left the field. He became so good at it that he could punt 40 to 50 yards. And with each punt he could make the ball go out of bounds inside the other team's 10-yard line. That took real skill.

Because of his many skills, Sam Baugh was a valuable player. During Sam's first 10 years with the Redskins, the team won five division titles and two NFL championships. And six times Sam led the NFL in passing. In 1945, he established an especially good passing record by completing better, than 7 out of every 10 passes that he threw. Sam Baugh could throw the ball overhand or sidearm at different speeds, for a long or short distance.

Sam played 16 years with the Redskins and finally retired in 1952. For many years after his retirement, Sam Baugh worked on his ranch in Texas. But football was still in his blood. In 1960 he was hired to coach the New York Titans of the newly formed American Football League (AFL). Two years later, he quit the Titans, and in 1964 he became head coach of the Houston Oilers. Sam Baugh's coaching career ended in 1967 when he retired to work full time on his ranch.

Over the years, many of the records Baugh set in football have been broken. This is because the professionals have followed the example Baugh set: they have made use of the forward pass as a scoring weapon. Today, the pros depend upon the forward pass completely.

Sid Luckman

Sid Luckman was one of the greatest distance passers in football. But his fame did not come from his ability to throw long passes. It came from making the T-formation popular. To this day, Sid Luckman is considered to be one of the smartest quarterbacks ever to have played pro football. It is said that he memorized 400 different plays. And he knew what each of the *other* 10 players on his team was supposed to do in each of those plays, too.

Sid Luckman was born in 1916 in Brooklyn, New York. He liked playing football as a child. When he started high school at 14, Sid made the football team. And a year later, he made the first string. During that time, Sid was not a good passer. But he was a shifty runner who could kick very well. He practiced often to improve his passing.

Sid graduated from high school with an outstanding football record. Because of this, many colleges offered him scholarships. Sid chose to go

to Columbia University, even though Columbia did not offer him a scholarship. The university found him a job instead, so that he could work his way through school.

At Columbia, Sid Luckman played on the football team. He was a good player, but the team did not win many games. Sid's football career would probably have ended after college if it had not been for one man—George Halas. Halas was owner and coach of the Chicago Bears pro football team. At the time he met Luckman, Halas was planning to use the T-formation in his games. The formation required a quarterback who was both smart and good at passing. When Halas saw Luckman play, he decided that Sid would be his quarterback.

Sid himself had no plans to continue his football career. His father had lost his trucking business during the Depression. So Sid felt he should go to work after college to help his family. But Halas lured him into the Chicago Bears club with a $10,000 contract, and Luckman accepted it.

In 1939, his first year with the Bears, Luckman played as a running back. At the same time, he learned the duties of the T-formation quarterback. One year later, he became the quarterback, and pro football has never been the same since.

Sid Luckman was a born quarterback. Not only

A happy Sid Luckman (right) signs his contract as Chicago Bears owner, George Halas, looks on.

was he a great passer, but he could also call the right plays. He was really good at handling the ball, too. His fake handoffs often fooled the defense.

As Halas had hoped, Luckman was the perfect quarterback for the T-formation. In 1940, Luckman led the Bears to the division title. Then came the NFL championship game against the Washington Redskins and their great quarterback, Sammy Baugh.

The game was a battle between the two great passers, Baugh and Luckman. It was also a test of the new T-formation. When the game ended,

19

Luckman and his Bears had won 73-0! After that, football teams all over the country started using the T-formation. But not every team had Sid Luckman to direct it.

Sid led the Bears to two more championships — in 1941 and 1943 — before going into the Merchant Marines in 1944. When he returned to the Bears in 1946, Sid had not lost his winning touch. That year, he directed Chicago to another championship. The 1946 championship title was the last of his career, for Sid Luckman retired after the 1950 season. In retirement, Luckman spent a lot of time teaching the T-formation to quarterbacks on college teams.

During the 12 years he played for the Bears, the handsome, intelligent Luckman was named all-league quarterback five times. In 1943 he was selected Most Valuable Player. That same year, Luckman set a record for touchdown passes in a single game. This happened on November 14, when the Bears were playing in New York. The New York fans held a Sid Luckman Day to honor the football star from Brooklyn. That day on the field, Sid threw seven touchdown passes — a record that has since been tied but not broken.

Over the years, Sid Luckman and George Halas have remained good friends. When Luckman has

time, he still coaches for the Bears. He travels with them when they play out-of-town games, and he often visits them at practice.

Sid Luckman's use of the T-formation made the Bears a winning team in the 1940s. Since that time, the Chicago Bears have never been as great as they were when Sid Luckman was their quarterback.

Bob Waterfield

Bob Waterfield was the most well rounded of all the great quarterbacks. He was capable of passing, kicking, and running with great skill. It was Waterfield who made the long, high-arching pass an important part of pro football. During his eight short years in professional football, Waterfield did not set any passing records. But few quarterbacks have been his equal in all-around ability.

Bob Waterfield was born in Elmira, New York, in 1920. A few years later, his family moved to Van Nuys, California. There Bob attended school. When he entered high school, Bob was small for his age. Year after year he tried to make the football team, but he did not make it until his senior year. Even then, Bob was not a good enough player to attract any college scholarship offers. But his mother wanted him to go to college. She finally talked him into it after he had worked for two years in an airplane factory. During those two

years, Bob continued to practice kicking and passing a football.

In 1940, Waterfield entered the University of California at Los Angeles (UCLA). He did not try out for the football team that first year. But he would sometimes drop by at football practice and work on his kicking. Waterfield's booming punts soon attracted the attention of the football coaches, and they invited him to try out for the team. When he did try out, the coaches were surprised to see that he could pass a football with accuracy. Because he had this skill, Bob Waterfield made the UCLA team as a quarterback. In 1942 he became a star player, leading UCLA to the Pacific Coast Conference championship.

In 1943 Bob went into the army and was sent to a training school for officers. But a year later, he got a bad knee injury, so the army had to let him go. Waterfield then returned to UCLA and played one more good season of football.

The Cleveland Rams, a new team in pro football, signed Waterfield to a contract for the 1945 season. That year, Bob was the star of the league as he led the Rams to the division championship. Then came the playoff game for the NFL title. In it, the Rams played the Washington Redskins. Beginning quarterback Waterfield completed 14 out of 27 passes that day. The Rams won, 15-14, over the Redskins.

For the first time in NFL history, a first-year player—Waterfield—was chosen Most Valuable Player in the league. The owner of the Rams was so impressed with his quarterback that he signed Waterfield to a three-year, $60,000 contract.

Before the start of the 1946 season, the Cleveland Rams moved west to become the Los Angeles Rams. The team played three seasons in Los Angeles without winning a division title. But in 1949, 1950, and 1951, the Rams won Western Division championships. In 1951, they went on to win the NFL title by defeating the Cleveland Browns, 24-17.

Bob Waterfield was a successful quarterback. But he was never very popular with the Los Angeles fans. He was a quiet man who did not attract much attention. It was his wife, actress Jane Russell, who was better known than he. Sportswriters often called him "The Great Stone Face" because there was never much of an expression on his face.

Waterfield played only one more season after 1951, sharing the quarterback duties with Norm Van Brocklin. Then he retired from football and tried a career in the movies. But his heart was still with football, and he soon returned to the Rams as an assistant coach. In 1960 he was named head coach. It was a hard job to fill because the Rams were not doing well at that time. Bob coached them through three bad seasons. Then he quit football to work for a motion picture company that he and his wife owned.

Bob Waterfield enjoyed a remarkable eight-year playing career. He led the NFL in passing two times, in kicking field goals three times, and in kicking extra points four times. He also did the Rams' punting—twice he punted for 88 yards. And he played defense as well as offense. By the end of his career, Waterfield had become one of the best pass defenders in the league.

Along with his other skills, Bob was a master ball handler. At times, he would fake a handoff to one of his running backs and then run with the ball himself. Often when he did this, he fooled not only the other team but also the officials.

Because of his many contributions to the sport of professional football, Bob Waterfield was elected to the pro football Hall of Fame. During his eight seasons, he guided the Rams to four division titles and two NFL championships. Los Angeles has not enjoyed such success in the years since then.

Otto Graham was such a gifted man that he might have had a successful career in any number of professions. But perhaps no career could have been as successful for him as his 10 years of professional football turned out to be. Graham was not a record-breaking passer. Nor was he a colorful performer. But no other quarterback in the history of the game led his team to more wins than did Otto Graham. In each of his 10 pro seasons, Graham led the Cleveland Browns into the league championship game. The Browns won 7 of those 10 games.

Otto Graham was born in Waukegan, Illinois, in 1921. His father had once been a pitcher in semi-professional baseball. But he had later become a music teacher at a Waukegan high school. Otto's mother was also a music teacher. If Otto had not had great athletic abilities, he probably would have found a career in music. He and his three brothers all played musical instruments.

As a boy, Otto's time was split between athletics and music. In high school he became a star in track, basketball, and football, though football was not one of his favorite sports. Otto was also an excellent student, and he received scholarship offers from several colleges.

After graduating from high school, Otto entered

Northwestern University on a basketball scholarship. At Northwestern, he wanted to study music and play basketball. Otto did not try out for the football team. But he did play football as part of the school's physical education program. Graham played so well that word got to the varsity coaches, and they talked him into trying out for the football team. He easily made the team, but a knee injury kept him from playing the first year.

In 1941, Otto Graham played on Northwestern's varsity football team and set a number of college records in passing. During his senior year, Graham was named Most Valuable Player in the Big Ten Conference. He was also named to most of the All-America football teams and to several All-America basketball teams as well.

When Graham left Northwestern in 1944, he entered the navy. Like other college football players in military service at the time, Graham played for a service football team. There he drew the attention of Paul Brown, a man who was planning to put together a new football team for the All-America Football Conference. Brown offered Graham a nice contract to play on his new team. Graham needed the money because he wanted to get married, so he signed with the team that came to be known as the Cleveland Browns.

Cleveland, with Otto Graham as quarterback, played its first game in the All-America Football Conference in 1946. But the Browns turned out to be too good for the conference. They won the title that year, and held it for the next three years. At the end of the 1949 season, the All-America Football Conference broke up. The unbeatable Cleveland Browns then became part of the National Football League.

The NFL was considered to be the best league in the country. But its fans looked down on the Cleveland team. They thought the Browns were a weak team that would suffer at the hands of the older NFL teams. And they often criticized Graham

Otto Graham carries the ball against the Los Angeles Rams in the 1950 NFL championship game.

Graham at the bottom of the heap, still clutching the ball

because he was the leader of the Browns.

In their first NFL game, the Cleveland Browns had to play defending champion Philadelphia. Otto Graham completed 21 out of 38 passes for 346 yards and 3 touchdowns as the Browns beat the Philadelphia Eagles, 35-10. Cleveland went on to win the conference title and the NFL championship.

Over the next five seasons, Otto led the Browns to their division title and then into the NFL championship playoff games. Two of those play-offs they won. But the pressure of being the team leader began to wear on Graham, and he retired at the end of the 1954 season.

At the start of the 1955 season, the Browns were helpless without Graham. So Paul Brown talked him into coming back. That year, Graham led Cleveland to another division title. In the league championship game, he threw two touchdown passes and scored two touchdowns himself as the Browns beat the Los Angeles Rams, 38-14. After that winning season, Otto Graham retired for good.

Otto Graham was as fine a person off the field as he was on the field. As a member of the Fellowship of Christian Athletes, he often spoke to young people about religion. Otto himself was a very religious man who did not drink or smoke.

Otto Graham left football at the peak of his career. Although he had set no great records, he had completed over half (55.7 percent) of all the passes he had thrown in his career. This passing record was very close to the record established by the great Sammy Baugh.

Norm Van Brocklin

Norm Van Brocklin may have been one of the greatest long-distance passers in pro football. But it is not for his passing ability that he is remembered. Van Brocklin became known as the most hot-tempered quarterback — and later, coach — that football has ever known. When things did not go his way, Van Brocklin could be very unpleasant. He especially hated to lose. When he did lose, he took his anger out on those around him. His teammates, as well as the men he coached, either hated or respected him.

Norm Van Brocklin was born in Eagle Butte, South Dakota, in 1926, the eighth child in a family of nine. When Norm was three years old, his family moved to Walnut Creek, California, and there Norm went to school. In high school, Norm was not especially good at sports. Nor was he a good enough student to receive a college scholarship. So after graduating from high school, he went into the navy.

In 1946, when his navy duty was over, Van Brocklin enrolled at the University of Oregon. He tried out for the football team and just barely made it. Norm was a very slow runner and was therefore of little use to the football team. A year later, however, Oregon started using the T-formation, a play that called for a good passer. Norm was the best passer on the team, so he not only became useful but also turned out to be the team's most important player. In 1948, Norm led Oregon to an almost unbeaten season. The team lost only to Southern Methodist University in the Sugar Bowl.

Van Brocklin finished college a year later, in 1949. Soon after that, he was selected to join the Los Angeles Rams pro football team. When he arrived at the Rams' training camp, Norm found that there were already three other quarterbacks on the team. One of them was the great Bob Waterfield. In time, two of the team's four quarterbacks were traded away, so Van Brocklin and Waterfield were left to share quarterback duties.

During his first two seasons with the Rams, Van Brocklin proved just how good he was. In 1950, he led the National Football League in passing. In 1951, he and Waterfield carried the Rams into the NFL championship game against the Cleveland Browns. That was an exciting game. In the fourth quarter the score was tied when Norm threw a 73-yard touchdown pass that won the game.

After the 1952 season, Waterfield retired. The Rams then hired Billy Wade, an outstanding college quarterback. By 1955 the Rams coach was once again using two quarterbacks—Van Brocklin and Wade. This angered Van Brocklin. But his anger did not stop the coach from using Wade even more often the following season.

At the start of the 1957 season, Norm was finally given the job of first-string quarterback. But he was upset by the fact that the coach sent the plays in from the bench instead of counting on *him* to call the plays. At season's end, Van Brocklin asked to be traded to another pro team.

The Rams traded Van Brocklin to the Philadelphia Eagles for the 1958 season. The Eagles were a poor team, winning only two games during Van Brocklin's first season. But Van Brocklin decided to change all that. As the quarterback, he *drove* the players into competition. By the end of the 1959 season, Philadelphia had finished in second place in its division. A year later, in 1960, Van Brocklin led the Eagles all the way to the NFL championship. For this achievement he was named Most Valuable Player in the NFL. Then suddenly, at the peak of his career, Van Brocklin quit as a player to become head coach of the Eagles. But Philadelphia wanted him to play as well as coach. Van Brocklin said no. Instead, he became head coach of the Minnesota Vikings, a new team in the NFL.

Van Brocklin as coach of the Minnesota Vikings

As a coach Norm Van Brocklin drove the Vikings with the same fury and temper he had used on his teammates when he was a quarterback. Although Minnesota won a few difficult games, the team did not finish any of its seasons with a very good record. Besides that, Van Brocklin did not get along with the Viking quarterback, Fran Tarkenton. In 1965, after a disappointing loss to Baltimore, Norm got into a "quitting match" with Tarkenton. Both said they were going to quit, but neither one of them did. Finally, Tarkenton resigned and, shortly after that, so did Van Brocklin. In 1968, Van Brocklin was named head coach of the Atlanta Falcons. He led the Falcons for six years, but left after the 1974 season.

In his playing days, Norm Van Brocklin led the NFL in passing for 3 years of his 12-year career. He was without equal as a long passer—*and* as the most hot-tempered player in the game.

Y. A. Tittle

A quarterback who does not play on a champion-ship team really has to be good in order to become a star. That's what happened to Y. A. Tittle, and he became one of the best quarterbacks of all time. Playing on a non-championship team was only one of the problems Tittle had to overcome. Tittle did not even *look* like a football player. And his name was so unusual that it brought smiles to people's faces.

Yelverton Abraham Tittle, Jr., was born in the small railroad town of Marshall, Texas, in 1926. Because Tittle had such a long, unusual name, people simply called him "Y. A." As for looks, Tittle had big ears and a large thin nose. He started to get bald rather early in his life, too.

Even as a child, Y. A. loved football. Along with the other kids in Texas, Y. A. almost worshipped the great quarterback Sam Baugh—another Texan. As Baugh had done in his youth, Y. A. hung a tire from a tree and practiced throwing passes through it. Y. A. also got some help from his older brother in learning how to hold and throw a football.

By the time Y. A. entered high school, he had become very good at throwing a football. He was so good that he was made the main ball handler for the school football team. In his senior year, he was named to the All-State team. But he was not scouted by college teams as much as other high-school stars were. Y. A. did turn down several offers, however, before he enrolled at Louisiana State University in 1944. A year later, Y. A. made the varsity football team. He became quarterback for the new T-formation play that the school was just starting to use.

For three seasons, Y. A.'s passing ability gave Louisiana State a lot of wins. But Y. A. always seemed to be playing in the shadow of other big-name stars. He did not even make the All-America team. The only notice he got in his senior year was for his performance in a game against Mississippi. In that game, Tittle intercepted a pass and had an open field in which to run for the goal post. As he ran for the goal line to score what would have been the winning touchdown, his pants fell down and he was caught from behind.

Even though Y. A. Tittle did not receive the notice that other college stars got, his skills as a quarterback did not go unnoticed by professional ball teams. After finishing college, Tittle was signed to a pro contract by the Cleveland Browns of the All-America Football Conference (AAFC). But just before training time, the Browns gave him to the Baltimore Colts. The Colts were the weakest team in the AAFC.

Y. A. Tittle (Number 14) suffered a cheekbone fracture on this play in 1953.

Playing with the Colts, Y. A. Tittle became the AAFC's Rookie of the Year in 1948. But despite Tittle's excellent performance, the Colts did not develop into a strong team. They performed so badly that people no longer came to see them play. So in 1950, the Baltimore Colts and several other teams in the AAFC were taken into the older and stronger National Football League. That season, the Colts won only 1 out of 12 games. A year later, the team broke up. The players went to other teams, and Tittle went to the San Francisco 49ers, where he stayed for 10 years.

During his years with San Francisco, Tittle led the 49ers to many near-championship wins. In 1953, the 49ers lost only three games, two of them while Y. A. was out with a broken cheekbone. In 1957, the 49ers were tied with Detroit at season's end for the league lead. But Detroit won the playoff game.

During the 1960 season, Tittle suffered injuries that affected his job as quarterback. San Francisco decided they could do without him, so Tittle was traded to the New York Giants in 1961. Tittle was then 35 years old. And he was suffering pain from the many injuries he had received over the years. But in his next years with the Giants, Y. A. Tittle was to win his greatest fame.

When he reported to the Giants, Y. A. was a lonely, unhappy man. Not only was he upset at having to leave the 49ers, but he was also unsure about his future with the Giants. The team already had a popular quarterback, Charlie Conerly. And the players were not at all friendly toward Tittle. But during the second game of the season, Conerly was hurt, and Y. A. was sent in as quarterback. Tittle completed 10 of 12 pass attempts to lead the Giants to victory.

After that game, Y. A. Tittle led the Giants to victories week after week. In that time, he won the

Tittle (left) and coach Allie Sherman watch the action on the field.

respect of both the players and the fans. New York finished the season by winning the division championship, which was Tittle's first. But the Giants lost to Green Bay in the NFL title game.

With Y. A. throwing both short passes and his famous long, high-arching bombs, New York won its division title for three straight years. But each year, they lost the league championship game.

Tittle's greatest game during those three years happened in 1962, when the Giants played the Washington Redskins. Y. A. completed 27 out of 39 passes for 505 yards and 7 touchdowns. (No professional quarterback has thrown more than 7 touchdowns in a single game.) A year later, Tittle threw a season total of 36 touchdown passes. This is a season record that is still unbroken and will be hard to beat.

In 1964, after winning three straight division titles—but no NFL championship titles—the Giants began to fall apart. Y. A. was always bothered by injuries. And he seemed to be losing his skill with the football. Y. A. Tittle retired after the 1964 season. When he left pro football, he took with him almost every passing record in the book. During his 17-year career, Y. A. Tittle completed more passes and more touchdown passes than his boyhood hero, Sammy Baugh.

Some football experts have said that Tittle was really not so great. The reason they give is that Tittle was never quarterback of an NFL championship team. Yet Tittle was named the NFL's Most Valuable Player three times. And in 1970, he was elected to the Hall of Fame.

Johnny Unitas

Johnny Unitas' rise to greatness in pro football is a story of hard work and constant effort. At the start of his career, Johnny had problems. But through hard work and the strong wish to be a professional football player, Unitas made quite a name for himself. He could really pass a football well. He was also known for his daring play calls and his wild, last-minute efforts to score.

Johnny Unitas was born in Pittsburgh, Pennsylvania, in 1933. His father, who owned a coal delivery business, died when John was just four. So Mrs. Unitas had to go to work to support her family. She took over her husband's business and studied at night to become a bookkeeper. All the while she worked, Mrs. Unitas was busy looking after her four children. It was her example that had much to do with Johnny's success. He always said that it was his mother who taught him the most about hard work.

In high school, Johnny Unitas was a tall, thin

boy who played end on the football team. Once, when the regular quarterback was injured, the coach tried Johnny in the quarterback position. Johnny did a fine job and went on to become an outstanding long passer. In his last year in high school, Unitas was asked to join the league All-Star team. Because of his athletic ability, Johnny hoped he could get a college scholarship.

None of the big colleges was interested in a tall, 170-pound quarterback, however. They thought Unitas was too light to play. But when Johnny was offered a scholarship from the University of Louisville (Kentucky), he took it. Louisville was a small school with a bad football team. The team didn't win many games while Unitas was there. But at Louisville, Johnny developed into an even better passer than he had been in high school. By the time he left Louisville, Unitas was ready for the professionals.

In the 1955 pro draft, the Pittsburgh Steelers picked Unitas on the ninth round. But the Steelers did not use him in the pre-season games. Before the regular football season started, Unitas was released from the team. At the same time, Unitas had other worries. His wife was going to have a baby, and money was becoming a big problem. John couldn't try out with another team because it was too late in the year to do that. So instead, he took a job with a construction company. In his time off, he played football for $6 a game with a semi-pro team in Pittsburgh. But he would not give up his dream of making it into the National Football League.

In an effort to get on a team, he called the Cleveland Browns about a tryout for the following

season. But before the tryout was arranged, the Baltimore Colts invited Unitas to come and show them what he could do. (The Colts team had broken up in 1951, but by 1955 it had been reorganized.) When they saw him perform, the Colts were impressed enough to give him a $7,000 contract. This happened at the start of the 1956 season. Johnny played only part time that year, and he did not have a very good season.

Two years later, in 1958, the boy who would not give up his dream became the sensation of professional football. His passing helped carry the Colts first to a division title and then to the NFL championship game against the New York Giants.

That game is remembered as one of the greatest football games ever played. In the last quarter, the Giants were leading Baltimore, 17-14. Then, with just two minutes left in the game, the Colts got the ball on their own 14-yard line. Time and again Unitas threw passes that steadily brought Baltimore upfield. The clock ticked away the time, but Unitas did not hurry. He carefully guided the Colts to within field goal range. The Colts scored the field goal and tied the score, sending the game into sudden-death overtime.

In the overtime period, Unitas continued to march the Colts toward the Giant's goal line. When they reached the New York 8-yard line, Unitas knew that running plays could set up an easy field goal and win the game. But he chose to pass to the 1-yard line and try for a touchdown. On the next attempt, Alan Ameche, the great fullback, went over the top for the touchdown that won the game.

That game, more than any other, showed Johnny Unitas' great abilities. He was one of football's greatest long passers. But he could move his team with short passes as well. He was always so cool under pressure that he was nicknamed "The Iceman." To the opposition, he seemed most dangerous in the final minutes of a game when his team was behind by only a few points. It was during those unlikely moments that Unitas always managed to score a win.

The Baltimore Colts won the NFL title again in 1959. But after that, John suffered the first in a series of injuries. With Unitas out of the game for a while, the Colts did not do well. In fact, they were in a slump for the next four seasons. It wasn't until 1964 that the Colts got their old energy back and won another division title. But they lost that year's championship game to the Cleveland Browns. A year later, Unitas suffered a bad knee injury that kept him out of the game for several weeks. The Colts competed for the division title without Unitas,

but they lost it to the Green Bay Packers.

The Packers were the Colts' main rivals again in 1966. That year, Unitas broke two of Y. A. Tittle's career records. He completed his 213th touchdown pass and gained more than 28,339 yards in passing. But in spite of these records, the team fell into a slump. The 1966 season turned out to be a bad one for the Colts.

The 1967 season was better, though. The Colts lost only one game all season. Unfortunately, it was the championship game that they lost. Unitas, however, threw more passes in 1967 than he did during any other time in his career. And he completed almost 59 percent of them, his best percentage yet. The NFL named Unitas its most valuable player that year. Then in 1968, Unitas suffered a bad arm injury that kept him out of the game for most of the season. But the Colts won the NFL championship playoff without him.

The Baltimore Colts went to the third annual Super Bowl game in 1969 against the New York Jets. Unitas, still not fully recovered from his arm injury, was sent into play late in the game. He fired up the team to score a touchdown—their only touchdown of the game. But he was not in good enough shape to lead the Colts back to victory. They were beaten by the Jets.

The 1970 pro football season was Unitas' last really successful time on the field. The Colts faced the Dallas Cowboys that year in the Super Bowl. Though the Colts won, Unitas was badly injured during the game. After that, he was in and out of the Baltimore line-up with injuries. In 1973, the Colts traded Unitas to the San Diego Chargers.

In the summer of 1974, Unitas called it quits. During his 18 years in pro football, he received more awards and set more records than any other American quarterback. Unitas may well be remembered as the greatest quarterback in football history.

Bart Starr

Bart Starr was the sensational quarterback of the Green Bay Packers during their winning seasons in the 1960s. During those years, the Packers were said to be the best team in professional football. They won two Super Bowl games, five league championships, one division title, and six conference titles.

Bart Starr was born in Montgomery, Alabama, in 1934. He and his younger brother grew up on a military base where their father was in the army. The two brothers liked sports, and they were both quite active.

Bart went out for many sports, especially football. But he did not really seem like the kind of person who played football. Bart was a shy, polite boy who seemed too nice for that rough game. In high school, he was a good, but not outstanding, quarterback.

In 1952, Starr enrolled at the University of Alabama and made the football team. He played very well during his first two years. But in his

Bart Starr (Number 15) gets some advice from Green Bay coach Vince Lombardi.

third year at Alabama, Starr suffered a back injury and missed much of the football season. Then, in his last year at Alabama, a new coach took over the team. The coach liked to use only the team's younger players. So Bart sat on the bench most of that year. The bench was a bad place for a player who wanted the pro scouts to see him play.

In the pro football draft of 1956, Bart Starr was almost overlooked completely. He was finally selected by the Green Bay Packers on the 17th round. The Packers had four other quarterbacks, so Bart was not very active that season. Over the next three seasons, Bart played in a few games but did not impress anyone.

Those years, 1956 to 1959, were bad ones for the Packers. They finished in last place every year. Then, in 1959, Vince Lombardi became the Green Bay coach, and things began to change for the Packers. At first, Lombardi felt that Starr was too nice and polite to be a tough leader on the field. When the season started, he had Bart playing third-team quarterback. But when Lombardi saw that the Packers were not doing well, he changed the line-up, giving Bart the first-team quarterback job. With Starr guiding them, the Packers won four of their five remaining games. And the next year, the Packers won the Western Conference title. They played the Philadelphia Eagles for the NFL championship, but they lost the game, 17-13.

The Packers went on to win the NFL championship in both 1961 and 1962. They did it with the help of Starr, a strong defense, and great running backs like Paul Hornung and Jim Taylor. In 1961 Bart played six games with a pulled muscle in his stomach. The Packers won five of those games. Then they went on to play the New York Giants in the championship game. In that game, Starr played better than the Giants' two great but aging quarterbacks, Y. A. Tittle and Charlie Conerly.

After winning the NFL title in 1961 and 1962,

the Packers lost the title to Chicago in 1963. That was the year running back Paul Hornung was out of the game. To some sports experts, this championship loss was proof that Starr could not win without all his great runners behind him. This idea was not widely accepted. But when Hornung returned to the line-up, the Packers again won two straight championships, in 1965 and 1966.

The truth of the matter was that, during both of those seasons, the Green Bay running attack had not been doing well. So the team had relied more and more on Bart's passing. This was plain to see in 1966 when the Packers played the Dallas Cowboys for the NFL championship. In that game, Starr completed 19 of 28 passes for four touchdowns, and the Packers won, 34-17. After seeing this, Starr's critics finally had to admit that they had been wrong about him.

In 1966, the first Super Bowl game was played between the champions of the National Football League and the American Football League. Green Bay's opponent was the Kansas City Chiefs, a team with a great defense. But Starr's passing overwhelmed the Chief's defense, and the Packers won, 35-10. Bart Starr was named Most Valuable Player in that game. He was also named Player of the Year in the NFL.

In 1967, without the help of Hornung and Taylor, Bart Starr led the Packers to a record third straight NFL title. The Packers went on to win another Super Bowl victory, this time over the Oakland Raiders. Starr retired as a quarterback in 1970 and became an assistant coach on the team. In 1975, Bart Starr was named the Packers' head coach.

Starr was never the showman that other great

Bart Starr in his office at home

quarterbacks were. But he did things many of them couldn't do. With his ability to read defenses, he could look over the defense and tell in a minute if he had called the right play in the huddle. If he hadn't, he would change the play while calling signals at the line of scrimmage. In some games, he changed as many as half of his plays in this way.

Bart Starr was a very accurate passer who was not often intercepted. He still holds the record for having thrown 294 passes without an interception. And of all the great quarterbacks, Starr had the highest career percentage of pass completions— more than 57 percent.

Lenny Dawson

Lenny Dawson was born to a family that could have fielded an entire football team. There were 11 children—eight boys and three girls. Since Lenny was the youngest of the boys, he had to learn to take care of himself. And he did, too.

Lenny Dawson was born in Alliance, Ohio, in 1935. As a boy, he developed some habits that were to cause him problems later in his football career. He became so independent and confident that he did not show much emotion. Some people took this to mean that Lenny did not have ambition or leadership ability. But this was not true.

As a boy, Dawson never cared much for football. He played the game just because his brothers did. Lenny didn't like the violence of football—he didn't enjoy being hit by other players. He did like other sports, though, especially baseball and basketball. By the time he started high school, Dawson had changed his mind about football. He tried out for the team and made it. In his senior

year, he was named to the All-State team in both basketball and football.

Dawson entered Purdue University in 1953 and became a star on the football team. From 1954 to 1956, he broke most of the passing records in the Big Ten Conference. One of the assistant coaches at Purdue during that time was Hank Stram. Later, Stram was to have great impact on Dawson's career in pro football.

Lenny Dawson left Purdue in 1957 and was the

first-round draft choice of the Pittsburgh Steelers. He played with Pittsburgh for three seasons, but during that time he didn't play often enough to work up a good sweat. The Pittsburgh coach thought Dawson did not have the desire to be a team leader. So he never gave Dawson many chances to prove himself.

Before the 1960 season started, Dawson was traded to the Cleveland Browns. But it was the same story there. The coach didn't understand Dawson and didn't think he had the ability to be a leader. As before, Dawson was not given many chances to perform on the field.

After Dawson had been with Cleveland for two years, everyone in the NFL gave up on him. Even Dawson was ready to quit the game. But things were soon to change for him, thanks to Hank Stram. Stram, Dawson's former college coach, was coaching the Dallas Texans of the newly formed American Football League. Stram remembered Dawson's great years at Purdue and wanted to give him a tryout with Dallas.

In 1962, after five years of sitting on the bench in the NFL, Lenny Dawson was released by Cleveland. No other team in the league claimed him, so he was free to try out with Stram's team. Dawson did not do well at first because he was rusty from not playing. But he practiced hard and finally made the team. During his first season, Dawson led the Texans to a championship title. Playing full-time for the first time in his pro career, he threw 29 touchdown passes. Over the season, he completed better than 60 percent of his passes. That year he was named the AFL's Most Valuable Player.

During the next three seasons, Lenny Dawson was one of the league's leading passers. But backers of the older and stronger NFL were knocking his success. They pointed out that even though Dawson was a star in the AFL, he had not been good enough to become a starting quarterback in the NFL.

A really good quarterback is hard to knock, however, regardless of the league he plays for. In 1966, Dawson led his team, now called the Chiefs, to the AFL championship title. (By 1966, the Texans had moved to Kansas City and became known as the Chiefs.) As the champions of the AFL, the Chiefs were scheduled to meet the champs of the NFL in the first Super Bowl game. That game pitted the Chiefs against the Green Bay Packers. But the Chiefs lost to the Packers, 35-10. Kansas City's loss, of course, only made the NFL backers believe even more that their league was better than the AFL. Lenny Dawson had to wait three years to show the NFL that they had

been wrong in not giving him a fair chance.

Three years later, during the 1969 season, Dawson was faced with a hard decision. He suffered a bad knee injury while the Chiefs were competing for another AFL title and a return to the Super Bowl. Surgery on the injured knee was recommended. But surgery meant that Dawson would miss the rest of the season. Dawson believed that the knee would improve without surgery. So he sat out several games in order to be in shape for the end of the season. If the Chiefs were going to the Super Bowl again, he wanted to be ready.

After missing several games, Dawson returned

to lead the Chiefs into the AFL playoffs, which they won. Now the Chiefs could look forward to their second Super Bowl. This time they were to meet the powerful Minnesota Vikings. Only a few days before the game, however, something happened that had serious meaning for Dawson. A TV network reported that Dawson was going to be called before the grand jury. This was going to happen, the report said, because Dawson had been betting on football games. Dawson said that he was not guilty of this serious charge. The whole incident brought great pressure on him, but in spite of it, Dawson led the Chiefs to a 23-7 win over the Vikings, As it turned out, Dawson was never called to appear before the grand jury.

The Super Bowl win was a great personal victory for Lenny Dawson. He had once been dropped by the NFL without being given a fair chance to show his ability. Now he had shown them how good he really was.

In 1970, 1971, and again in 1975, Lenny Dawson ranked among the leading passers in pro football. Then, at the end of the 1975 season, Lenny retired from the Chiefs. Like many former pros, he continued his involvement in football by becoming a sports commentator on radio and television. With 18 years of experience behind him, Lenny Dawson was a natural for the job.

Joe Namath will probably not be playing football long enough to break any of the great passing records. Repeated injuries to Joe's knees have been cutting short his playing season for the last few years. But even if he is forced to retire, Joe will be remembered for a long time to come. He is certainly one of the most colorful quarterbacks of all time. And he has also done the most toward giving the American Football League a new look.

These facts do not mean that Joe isn't a great quarterback. Some experts think he may rank among the two or three best. But Namath's activities outside of football have often overshadowed his playing accomplishments.

Joe Namath was born in 1943 in Beaver Falls, Pennsylvania, where his father worked in a steel mill. When Joe was a boy, his father took him to visit the mill. The steel mill was so hot, dirty, and noisy that Joe decided he would never work in such a place.

In his youth, Joe was a wild, tough kid who learned how to take care of himself. He especially liked sports. During his first year in high school, Joe tried out for the football team. But because he was small for his age, he was not accepted on the team. By the following year, Joe had grown 3 inches and had gained 25 pounds. He made the football team that year and also played baseball and basketball.

Joe Namath became an All-State quarterback in his last year of high school. As a result, many colleges tried to get him to enroll. Joe's choice was the University of Maryland, but his grades were not good enough for admission there. So he went to the University of Alabama instead.

Joe Namath became an outstanding football star at Alabama. But his wild, fun-loving way of life sometimes got him into trouble with his tough coach, Bear Bryant. Once when Joe was seen drinking in a bar, Bryant suspended him for the rest of the season. Joe had to sit on the sidelines while his Alabama teammates played in the Sugar Bowl. The incident almost caused him to quit school.

During Joe's last year at Alabama, he suffered a severe leg injury that has bothered him ever since. He played only part time that last season. But he still set many passing records.

Joe graduated from the University of Alabama in 1964. At that time, the National Football League and the newly formed American Football League were in a bidding war. Both leagues were trying to get the nation's best college players. And both leagues wanted Joe Namath. While the leagues competed with each other for Joe's signature on a contract, Joe took his time about making a decision. This kept the competition going. In the end, Joe signed with the AFL's New York Jets for the huge sum of $400,000. It was because of this deal that the two leagues later joined together into one league. That way, they wouldn't have to pay such

Joe Namath (left) fires off a pass, protected by the Jets offensive line.

large sums of money in competing against each other for players.

Joe Namath became a star even before he played his first pro football game. He had signed for more money than any other rookie had ever received before. And he had a reputation as a swinger, a young man who enjoyed being seen in fancy nightclubs with pretty women. Newspaper and magazine reporters wrote stories about everything he did.

Joe was not an instant success with the Jets, however. For the first five games of the 1965 season, he sat on the bench. But when he did get the chance to play, Joe showed everyone just how good he was. At season's end, he was named Rookie of the Year. Joe played the following 1966 season with another leg injury, one that required surgery when the season ended.

In 1967, Namath made the Jets happy that they had hired him. He passed for a total of 4,007 yards that season. It was something no other quarterback had ever done before in a single season. Even so, the Jets did not win the championship. The disappointed Jets' fans had been waiting for a championship title ever since Joe joined the team.

The Jets were in good shape in 1968, and Joe was playing better than ever. By using short, accurate passes along with his famous long bombs, Joe led the Jets to the Eastern Division title that year. Then they moved on to meet the powerful Oakland Raiders in the AFL championship game. The Jets upset the Raiders, 27-23. The stage was now set for the third Super Bowl game between the champions of the AFL and NFL.

In the two previous Super Bowls, the NFL team had won easily. So naturally, the backers of the NFL claimed that their league was far stronger than the AFL. When the sides were drawn—the New York Jets of the AFL vs. the Baltimore Colts of the NFL—the Colts were favored to win by

three touchdowns. Namath caused a stir by saying that his team was going to win. Nobody but Joe believed it.

Joe Namath was the master quarterback of the game. With a mixture of running and throwing long and short passes, he picked apart the Baltimore defense. The Jets surprised the sports world by winning the 1968 Super Bowl, 16-7. No longer was the AFL looked upon as weaker than the NFL.

Joe's football activities have always made the news, and so have his private activities. In 1969, Joe was involved in a dispute over a business dealing. At the time, he was part owner of a nightclub in New York City. The club was often visited by people who were thought to be lawbreakers. When this became known, the commissioner of the AFL demanded that Joe sell his ownership in the club. If he didn't, he wouldn't be allowed to play pro football. Joe answered by threatening to retire. But when he saw that his threat would not change the commissioner's mind, Joe sold his ownership in the club and rejoined the Jets.

Namath played for the Jets through the 1976 season when he was traded to the Los Angeles Rams. After one season with the Rams, he retired from football in 1977, then starred in a short-lived TV series, "The Waverly Wonders," in 1978.